W9-BLF-245

Please remember that this is a library book,
and that it belongs only temporarily to each
person who uses it. Be considerate. Do
not write in this, or any, library book.

Collaborative Practices for Educators
Strategies for Effective Communication

WITHDRAWN

Patty Lee, Ed.D.

Peytral Publications, Inc.

Minnetonka, Minnesota

Collaborative Practices for Educators Strategies for Effective Communication
by Patty Lee

Published by:

Peytral Publications, Inc.
P.O. Box 1162
Minnetonka, MN   55345
(952)949-8707 Fax (952)906-9777

371. 1022
L 477c
1999

All rights reserved. No part of this book may be used or reproduced in any manner without written permission from the publisher, except for brief quotations embodied in critical articles and reviews. Permission is granted to the purchaser to reproduce the "Tip Cards" for personal use only. Photocopying or other reproduction of this material for entire school districts, workshop participants, classes or inservice training is strictly prohibited.

Copyright ©1999 Peytral Publications, Inc. All rights reserved.
First Printing 1997
Second Printing 1999 revised
Printed and bound in the United States of America

Publisher's Cataloging in Publication
(Provided by Quality Books, Inc.)

Lee, Patty
        Collaborative practices for educators :
strategies for effective communication / Patty Lee. – Rev ed
        p.cm.
        LCCN: 99-70196
        ISBN 1-890455-26-1

        1. Teaching. 2. Communication in education. 3. Teaching teams.
        4. Team learning approach in education.   I. Title

LB1025.3.L44 1999   371.1'02
                             QBI99-251

Library of Congress Catalog Card Number 99-070196

TABLE OF CONTENTS

Section Five – Listening

WITHDRAWN

Section Six - Speaking Clearly

Tip Cards for Effective Collaboration

FOREWORD

WE are the resources for collaboration in today's schools. **WE** are the agents of change. No matter what innovation is challenging us, no matter what mandate is required, **PEOPLE** are at the center and **COMMUNICATION** is the foundation.

Why a Book About Collaboration?

Today's schools are being asked to become more inclusive in the education they provide. Students are coming to school with a variety of complex and unpredictable needs. Some of the learning models we have used in the past will not serve the needs of students for the future.

"Pull-out" programs have been found to be less than effective as students often fail to generalize the skills learned in segregated environments. We cannot afford to continue to create a new programs with new specialists for every learning need. We as educators must learn to work collaboratively, placing the students at the center of our efforts. In essence we must learn to "mind each other's business".

The word "Collaboration" is made up of two important parts. "Co" meaning "with" and "labor" meaning "work". Educators are being challenged to "work with" one another in new and sometimes difficult ways. The once sacred private space of a teacher's classroom is now often the domain of several educators at the same time. As the curriculum becomes more integrated, for example Spelling is not always separate from Mathematics or Social Studies curriculum, educators also need to become more integrated among themselves, working on common ground in the best interest of students.

This book is written to assist you in your collaboration with colleagues, parents, students, and administrators. The strategies and practices presented are drawn from over 30 years experience in the fields of general and special education. Teachers, paraprofessionals, specialists, parents, and students have contributed to the ideas by sharing their stories, suggestions, successes, and mistakes. As you try the strategies and practices in this book, you will become aware of which communi-cation skills you are naturally good at and the ones in which you need to improve. You will learn how to apply what you already KNOW to what you DO.

What is in this Book ?

This book is based upon the premise that we are often more collaborative with our students than we are with our adult colleagues. We use effective communication skills more naturally with our students than we may with the parents, paraprofessionals, and other teachers with whom we work. We listen more closely to students, we ask more meaningful questions, we attempt to understand where our students are "coming from", we put energy into explaining ourselves and we watch for indications of misunderstanding. On the other hand, we often are much more casual in our communication with adults. We may find ourselves interrupting more often, putting energy into getting our own point across rather than attempting to understand theirs, listening halfheartedly and not giving much thought to how we express ourselves. These are habits that occur frequently among adults who work together and they interfere with effective communication. When we are able to use the same communication skills with adult colleagues as we do with our students, we build the foundation for collaboration. This foundation is made up of six critical areas of effective communication:

1. Developing Expectations--Anticipating and predicting outcomes.

2. Preparing Ahead--Planning ahead and gathering resources to enhance the interaction.

3. Understanding Perspectives--Acknowledging, recognizing, and respecting a diversity of opinions.

4. Asking Questions--Inquiring and seeking more information.

5. Listening--Making a conscious effort to hear what is said.

6. Speaking Clearly--Sending a message that is received as it was meant.

One section is devoted to each of the above areas. The section begins by describing what we know about each of the preceding six areas and why the area is important for effective communication. The section continues by differentiating between the behaviors which occur with students in the classroom as compared to the behavior which may occur with adults. Following this comparison, ten strategies are listed that relate to each of the six areas. Within each of the ten strategies are three suggested practices for use in your educational setting. The practices are divided into those you can do on your own, with another person, and within a group setting. In all, the book includes 60 strategies and 180 practices to assist with improving your communication and in turn your collaboration.

How to Use This Book

The book is structured so that you can work on any of the six areas of communication and in any order you prefer. You can try some of the ideas by yourself, if you are not ready to try them with another person. You can suggest to your grade level or content area team that you practice some of the ideas together. You can focus on just one area of communication or several at once.

Some people learn best by keeping a journal or record of the prac-tices tried and the outcomes observed. It is helpful to record what you did, how you felt, and what you learned in the interaction. It is also important to note what worked and did not work for you. Do not expect to change all of your communication behaviors overnight. As with any meaningful change, it will take time and practice. Be patient with your-self and note the gradual shift to more satisfying and effective commun-ication.

The book is an exceptional resource to be used for staff develop-ment, or to incorporate into inservice training for educational teams. Educators can use this as a tool to discuss their current communication practices. Often by incorporating only a few of the changes, educational teams will note a significant improvement in group communication. The suggested practices can also be used as discussion starters and additional strategies may be designed which are specific to the particular school setting and current issues within the setting. Secondary and post secondary educators with find this book full of activities which can be adapted to help teach effective communication skills to students. The strategies and practices in this book are meant to be generic so they may lend themselves to application in all educational settings.

Section One

DEVELOPING EXPECTATIONS

You'll see it when you believe it

Wayne Dyer, 1989, Avon Books

DEVELOPING EXPECTATIONS

What We Know

To develop expectations is to anticipate, think ahead, and predict occurrences and outcomes.

★ Developing expectations gives us a sense of control and confidence in relationship to future events.

★ When we develop expectations, we become pro-active rather than reactive in our interactions.

★ Thinking ahead about communication with others can assist us in producing positive outcomes rather than leaving it to chance.

★ Predicting a variety of possible occurrences challenges us to generate a range of responses which can lead to increased flexibility.

★ Anticipating the dynamics of an interaction can increase our ability to be more accepting of differing points of view.

Developing Expectations – What We DO

In developing expectations

WHAT WE OFTEN DO with KIDS	WHAT WE SOMETIMES DO with ADULTS
Explain/Co-create classroom rules and standards of behavior	Conduct our meetings in ways they've always been conducted
Discuss and display ground rules for participation	Expect newcomers to "figure out" the ground rules; rely on "word of mouth"(informal means)
Consider time allotments for task completion; make assignments accordingly	Attempt to "fit" the task into a prescribed time slot
Determine what times of day will be best for what types of learning	Assume that the traditional time allotted is all we have
Assess the interpersonal dynamics for effective instructional grouping	Recognize, accept, and figure that "what you see is what you get"
Formulate student-teacher roles and responsibilities	Allow and let the traditional role (e.g. psychologist) determine the responsibilities (psychometric assessment)
Anticipate daily crises, interruptions, and delays	Expect the task (IEP staffing) to be completed within a predetermined time frame (1 hour)
Predict that we will need to accommodate for individual learning differences	Expect everyone to process information in the same way (our way)

Strategies for Developing Expectations

1. Develop an agreed upon set of ground rules for effective commun-ication or professional meetings.

2. Orient new members and visitors to ground rules.

3. Anticipate what people with different points of view might say and how you would respond.

4. State aloud what you believe you can or cannot accomplish in allotted amount of time.

5. Generate their expectations at the beginning of a meeting.

6. Establish regular times for reviewing roles and responsibilities.

7. Ask colleagues what they expect from students, from parents, and from you.

8. Keep a log (record) of communication interactions. Analyze the log for patterns and themes.

9. Visualize your next communication interaction as positive and produc-tive.

10. Anticipate potential communication breakdowns that could occur at work.

Strategies and Practices for Developing Expectations

Strategy 1   *Develop an agreed upon set of ground rules for effective communication at professional meetings.*

Individual

Note your own speaking and listening skills at meetings. What could you do differently at the next meeting that would improve your communication? Do it.

Colleague

Have a discussion with a colleague who attends the same meetings as you. Ask "What would improve our communication at these meetings?" Take the sugges-tions to the larger group.

Group

Have each person complete this sentence: "Our team communication would improve significantly if we ...". Post all responses on a flip chart and discuss which ones are "doable." Have each person rank their top 3 and total the rankings to obtain the top 3 for the entire group. Commit to doing these.

Strategy 2   *Orient new members and guests to ground rules.*

Individual

Take it upon yourself to meet with parents before an IEP staffing to inform them of what they can expect at the meeting (agenda, participants, and time frame). Distri-bute a copy of the agenda before the actual meeting.

Colleague

Most IEP meeting includes a guest (someone who does not attend such meetings on a regular basis such as parents, students, general education teachers, or a community representative). Select one person from the core team to handle introductions and to inform guests of the ground rules and typical process.

Group

With the consent of the group members, video or audio tape a typical meeting (faculty, team, or IEP) and have the video available for new staff to watch.

Strategy 3   **Anticipate what people with different points of view might say and how you might respond**.

Individual

Identify a colleague with whom you often disagree. Write 5 questions you could ask this person to get him/her to elaborate on an opinion.

Colleague

Interview two people with differing perspectives on an issue. During the interview make sure that you ask questions and refrain from making comments. Consider how you would mediate a discussion between these two people.

Group

Bring clarity to your own point of view by writing the specifics of how you feel, think, and believe about an issue. Now write how a person from an opposite point of view would feel, think, and believe.

Strategy 4 **State aloud what you believe you can or cannot accomplish in an allotted amount of time.**

Individual

When a colleague asks to speak to you are unable to give your full attention (e.g. in a hurry, preoccupied, or distracted) say something like, "I want to listen to what you're saying, and I'm unable to give you my full attention right now, so could we talk at a later time?"

Colleague

When you begin a planning session with a colleague, (e.g., developing a thematic unit for team-teaching) say something like, "I brought some materials, I'd like for us to see if we want to use. What do you want for us to accomplish in this session?"

Group

At the beginning of an IEP meeting, say something like "Today, we hope to review (student's) progress and make decisions about future services. We have about an hour to do this. If we don't accomplish what we need to in the allotted time, we'll schedule another session."

Strategy 5 **Have the group generate their expectations at the beginning of a meeting.**

Individual

Personally write what you expect will happen in the next interaction with a colleague; what he will say/do-what you will say/do. After the interaction, note in writing how accurate your predictions were.

Colleague

Prior to a parent-teacher conference, send a form asking the parent(s) to write three questions they have about their child's progress to bring the completed form to the conference. Ask the parents to read their questions at the beginning of the meeting. Write the questions on paper or a flip chart so they can be referred to through-out the conference.

Group

Each person attending the meeting writes one thing they hope to accomplish at the meeting. During the first five minutes read these aloud to see if you're on common ground.

Strategy 6 **Establish regular times for reviewing roles and responsibilities.**

Individual

At the beginning of the school year, write each of the roles you believe your job entails (teacher, consultant, parent, peer support, friend). Beside each of the roles, write the responsibilities that are inherent in that role.

Colleague

When teaming with a colleague, develop a calendar for the year that delineates periodic checkpoints to review responsibilities such as grading, contacting parents, disciplining, and communicating with other staff.

Group

On a quarterly basis, have the IEP team review indivi-dual roles in relation to the IEP meetings. Discuss joint responsibilities for communicating with parents, report-ing progress at staffings, using jargon free language, and preparing students to participate in IEP meetings.

Strategy 7	**Ask colleagues what they expect from students, from parents, and from you.**

Individual

Formulate several ways to ask colleagues what their expectations are, such as: "Tell me about how you run your classroom," and "What kind of contact would you like to have with parents?"

Colleague

Ask the questions from the previous Individual Practice Activity and listen carefully to the answer. Ask addi-tional questions to prompt your colleague to elaborate further, such as, "What have you found that doesn't work in your classroom?"

Group

At a faculty meeting discuss "How we would like our students to describe us." Then talk about what beha-viors on the part of the staff would lead to such descrip-tions and perceptions.

Strategy 8   Keep a record of communication interactions. Analyze the log for patterns and themes.

Individual   Keep a daily journal for one month, noting the colleagues with whom you interact. Are there some colleagues with whom you rarely communicate?

Colleague   Think of someone with whom you plan on a regular basis. Is the communication equal or is one person more dominant? Would you like for that to change?

Group   During a meeting, calculate the number of statements made compared to the number of questions asked.

Strategy 9   Visualize your next communication interaction as positive and productive.

Individual   Set a timer for five minutes. Write as quickly as you can the ways to communicate clearly. Don't concern yourself with spelling, punctuation, or duplication. After five minutes, read through the list and visualize the settings where you most often use these commun-ication abilities.

Colleague   Imagine you are in conversation with a colleague with whom you often disagree. Picture yourself as a good listener, taking into consideration your colleagues' point of view, and then clearly stating how you see the issue differently.

Group Visualize yourself with your own students presenting a lesson, clearly and with confidence. Now imagine the audience as a group of your peers and that your presentation continues to be clear and confident.

Strategy 10 **Anticipate potential communication breakdowns that could occur at work.**

Individual Think about a behavior of a colleague which you find irritating and "pushes your buttons". Examine what you typically do in response to this behavior. What might you do differently next time?

Colleague Ask a colleague to read a note you are planning to send home to parents. Ask your colleague to check for understanding (is it clear) and "user-friendliness."

Group Think about a recent meeting where communication broke down and you did not say anything. What do you wish you would have said? Imagine saying it next time.

Use this page to write down ideas that might come to mind while reading/referring to this guide.
Remember, collaboration begins with each one of us making ourselves accessible to others.

Section Two

PREPARING AHEAD

If you always do what you've always done, you'll always get what you've always gotten. Is it enough?

Author Unknown

PREPARING AHEAD

What We Know

To prepare ahead is to plan in advance what physical, mental, human, and material resources might be needed to increase the effectiveness of the upcoming lesson, meeting or interaction.

★   Preparing materials in advance reduces the likelihood we will have to take away from meeting time to get these materials.

★   Changing the physical arrangements can help prompt new ways of thinking. Arranging furniture ahead of time and in a variety of ways conveys that consideration has been given to the type of meeting.

★   Thinking ahead about the questions (not just the statements) we have assists us in creating a meaningful dialogue with our co-workers.

★   Preparing ahead, so the next meeting will be more effective than the last, increases the likelihood of positive change.

★   Planning ahead often results in a general sense of readiness among individuals.

Preparing Ahead – What We DO

In preparing ahead

WHAT WE OFTEN DO with KIDS	WHAT WE SOMETIMES DO with ADULTS
Decide/rehearse what to say	Say the first thing that comes to mind
Think about how to introduce an idea	Figure we'll begin the way we've always started
Prepare according to the learning outcomes we want	Disregard our desired outcomes (outcomes is to get it done)
Plan what questions to ask	Prepare what we'll say not what we'll ask
Select what materials will be used	Use the existing forms to guide the meeting
Consider possible room arrangements depending upon the lesson	Meet in the same arrangement time after time
Seek out human and material resources that will supplement (support) the lesson	Assume that routine members will be the only ones needed
Design practice activities to reinforce new skills	Assume we have the skills we need and there's no need for practice
Determine how to evaluate learning progress	Neglect to consider the learning progress of adult co-workers
Expect to monitor and respond to feedback from students so that we can improve the lesson	Persist in conducting business in habitual ways regardless of feedback

Strategies for Preparing Ahead

1. Establish a process where adults review and recommend the best places and room arrangements for meetings.

2. Develop the agendas for meetings based on colleagues questions and concerns.

3. Review on a regular basis team members' material and experiential resources.

4. Develop a process for observing and assessing "meeting" behaviors.

5. Review the purpose or intent of different types of meetings.

6. Set annual goals for the purpose of improving communication.

7. Devise methods of tracking progress on annual communication goals.

8. Establish practices for obtaining feedback from key consumers.

9. Create new ways to think about standard practices.

10. Use scheduled breaks during the year for predicting communication needs that might arise.

Strategies and Practices for Preparing Ahead

Strategy 1 the	*Establish a process where adults review and recommend best places and arrangements for meetings.*

Individual

Picture a recent meeting you were in. How was the room arranged? Could people see each other? What physical barriers interfered with communication? What could you do to improve the arrangement?

Colleague

Before your next meeting with a co-worker, choose a place that is different from where you typically meet. Think about ways to control possible distractions.

Group

After one of your standard meetings (e.g., child study meeting) ask members if the setting and arrangement are conducive to good communication. Encourage people to make suggestions.

Strategy 2 — *Develop agendas for meetings based on participants questions and concerns.*

Individual
What information would you like from a parent of one of your students? How could you ask questions that would elicit this information?

Colleague
Think about three ways to ask a colleague about their classroom management. Write down the questions. Plan to ask at least one of the questions the next time you meet.

Group
Ask faculty members to write a question for the entire faculty to discuss. Place the questions in a central location. Discuss 2 or 3 questions at each faculty meeting

Strategy 3 — *Review on a regular basis team members' material and experiential resources.*

Individual
Keep a listing of outside community resource people who might be available to help with creative programming for kids.

Colleague
After attending a workshop or conference, share the information with a colleague, highlighting the sessions that you attended. Offer to make copies of the information received. Find ways to share with entire faculty.

Group

Set aside one of your regularly scheduled team meetings to brainstorm the areas of competencies within the team (e.g. behavior management, cooperative learning). Post the list in a central location and update it at least twice a year.

Strategy 4	*Develop a process for observing and assessing communication which occurs during meetings.*

Individual

During a staffing, keep track of all of the abbreviations (IEP, OT, etc.) by writing them each time they are said. Was there anyone in the meeting who might not know what those abbreviations mean?

Colleague

Ask someone who does not regularly attend staffings (general education teacher, parent) what would improve communication and understanding at these meetings. Share these ideas with the rest of the team members.

Group

At every third staffing, designate one team member as "communication process observer." Decide as a team the communication behaviors the observer should watch for and record (e.g. interruptions, abbreviations, jargon, length and frequency of member talk). Discuss the results.

Strategy 5 of	Review the purpose or desired outcomes of different types meetings

Individual

Think about how you would like a parent to describe you after a parent conference. How might you behave so that the parent would describe you this way?

Colleague

With a colleague, before a planning session, individually write what you hope to accomplish at the session. Read the lists to each other. Prioritize the list together.

Group

In preparing for a committee or task force meeting, plan to ask everyone on the committee what they believe is the current task at hand. Discuss similarities and differences among responses.

Strategy 6	Set annual goals for the purpose of improving communication.

Individual

Ask yourself "What is one thing I could do now to significantly improve my communication?" Set a goal related to the behavior

Colleague

Discuss with a co-worker the current paperwork you are both doing. Could any of it be omitted, revised, or com-bined for efficiency and effectiveness? If so, set a timeline for making the changes or recommending the changes to the appropriate personnel.

Group

Ask the interdisciplinary staffing team to respond to a checklist of communication skills related to staffings (e.g., stating the purpose of the meeting, summarizing main points, checking for understanding). Set goals around the areas that members rank the lowest.

Strategy 7   *Devise methods of tracking progress in communication.*

Note: *These practices are directly related to the practices in strategy 6*

Individual

Once you have set a communication goal, write it. Devise a way to track daily the number of opportunities you had for practice and then the number of times you actually prac-ticed the new behavior.

Colleague

After any new form of paperwork is developed, ask the key people (those who will use the form), for feedback on its readability and clarity.

Group

Post the goals you set in Group Activity of Strategy 6 in a prominent place where you typically hold interdisciplinary staffings. Review your progress at least three times a year.

Strategy 8 *Establish practices for obtaining feedback from key consumers*

Individual Discuss with your students how they view you as a listener. What do they think you could improve?

Colleague When you present with a colleague (to the faculty, at a conference) decide together the type of feedback desired and how the information will be obtained.

Group Ask parents and regular educators to evaluate the interdisciplinary staffing process from their points of view. What would they suggest for improving communication and making the process more "user-friendly."

Strategy 9 *Create new ways to think about standard practices.*

Individual The next time you get an unexpected "free" hour (an appointment is canceled, a meeting is postponed, etc.) fill the free hour with something you love to do.

Colleague Think of five people with whom you work on a daily basis. Designate Monday for one, Tuesday for another, etc. On each day of the following week, make sure that you connect with that day's person in a meaningful way.

Group Conduct your next committee, planning, staffing, or faculty meeting off school grounds.

> ## Strategy 10 *Use scheduled breaks in the year for predicting communication needs that will arise.*

Individual

At the end of the first quarter of school think about the way you could arrange the chairs and tables differently for parent conferences. Consider an arrangement that would facilitate effective communication.

Colleague

Meet with a colleague for breakfast or lunch during one of your school breaks. Discuss what you believe will come up during second semester that will need good, clear communi-cation.

Group

As an interdisciplinary staffing team, discuss a potentially difficult staffing that is scheduled in the future. Brainstorm ideas for creating as collaborative a climate as possible.

Use this page to write down ideas that might come to mind while reading/referring to this guide.
Remember, collaboration begins with each one of us making ourselves accessible to others.

Section Three

UNDERSTANDING PERSPECTIVES

There is nothing so unequal as the equal treatment of unequals.

Author Unknown

UNDERSTANDING PERSPECTIVES

What We Know

To understand perspectives is to acknowledge that everyone sees the world through his own view and to recognize that comprehending those diverse views will serve communication in positive and productive ways.

★ Understanding perspectives conveys respect and opens the lines of communication.

★ Taking diverse perspectives into account during problem solving increases the possibility of developing mutually satisfying outcomes.

★ Utilizing multiple perspectives can result in creating a variety of new responses and alternatives that would not be available from any single perspective.

★ Considering other perspectives and responding accordingly is simply "treating others as we would like to be treated ourselves."

Understanding Expectations-What We DO

In understanding other perspectives

WHAT WE OFTEN DO with KIDS	WHAT WE SOMETIMES DO with ADULTS
Recognize that they'll have a bad day now and then	Act like everyday is about the same
Accept that their emotional state will affect their productivity	Expect about the same productivity across time
Ask how they are when we perceive they're troubled	Avoid interacting or bringing up that they might be troubled.
Cut them some slack when we know of difficult circumstances in their lives	Expect them to leave their difficulties at home
Respond with empathy to a tough situations	Mind our own business
Accept that kids are at varying levels of skill development. What is hard for one may be easy for another	Expect adults to be similarly competent, confident, and productive
Demonstrate patience when they're trying something new	Fail to recognize they might be trying something new
Ask questions to determine "where they're coming from"	Make assumptions about "where they're coming from"
See it as a positive challenge when they disagree with us	Take it personally when they disagree with us

Strategies for Understanding Perspectives

1. Develop ways to encourage others to explain their perspectives.

2. Listen actively to people who have differing perspectives.

3. Learn about differences in adult learning styles.

4. Develop habits that increase understanding and decrease judgment.

5. Develop ways of thinking and speaking that are inclusive rather than exclusive.

6. Become a good observer of people.

7. Increase awareness of "self talk".

8. Read with the purpose of understanding opposing points of view on a controversial issue.

9. Develop new ways to get to know people.

10. Discover the importance of silence.

Strategies and Practices for Understanding Perspectives

Strategy 1	***Develop ways to encourage others to explain their perspectives***

Individual

Think about things people do and say that encourage you to explain your perspective. Write these down. Add to the list as you hear other examples.

Colleague

The next time someone is expressing a perspective different from your own, urge them to elaborate.

Group

At a team meeting, bring in someone who is not regularly on the team (e.g. a parent). Ask that person to give you their perspective on whatever issue you've been dealing with (e.g. student portfolios).

Strategy 2   *Listen actively to people who have differing perspectives*

Individual   Listen to a talk show host whose beliefs are usually opposite from yours. Write down what you would say in a debate with this person

Colleague   When conversing with a colleague who often has a different point of view, ask a question directly linked to what they just said.

Group   Ask each person in the group finish a sentence such as, "Our group would function better if we_____." As each person shares their response, compare the similarities and differences.

Strategy 3   *Learn about adult learning and communication styles.*

Individual   Check bookstores and libraries for information on Adult Learning Styles. Popular authors include Gregorc, Kersey, Kolb, Myers-Briggs. Fill out one of the questionnaires. Read the authors' interpretation. Reflect on how you come across to others.

Colleague   Identify a co-worker who you think has a different style than yours. Read about the values, preferences, and behaviors of that style. How do you see those character-istics in your co-workers' daily behaviors?

Group

See if your faculty or team would be interested assessing learning styles together. Arrange for all members to take the inventory, assess the groups' strengths and weak-nesses, and discuss the type of implications the results may have in day to day communication.

Strategy 4	***Develop habits that increase understanding and decrease judgment***

Individual

When you're just about the change a radio or TV station because you don't like what's on, listen or watch for one more minute. With as much neutrality as possible, imagine who would like this and why?

Colleague

The next time a colleague suggests an idea you don't think will work, ask the person to tell you more. As they elabor-ate, listen with the intention of fully understanding the idea.

Group

Ask each person in the group (faculty, team, committee) to bring a childhood photo of themselves and share a "story" from that part of their life.

Strategy 5   *Develop ways of thinking and speaking that are inclusive rather than exclusive*

Individual

Before meeting with a team member about a student you have in common, make a list of all the things you both probably want for the student.

Colleague

When exchanging ideas with a colleague, try replacing the word "but" with the word "and." For example: instead of saying "That's a good idea, but" say "That's a good idea, and I'm concerned about ..."

Group

When planning an IEP staffing, ask each person to think of someone, who is not a regular member, whom you could invite to help solve the problem.

Strategy 6   *Become a good observer of people*

Individual

Immediately following a stressful interaction at work, write down all the feelings you had during the interaction. Reflect on your behaviors. What did you do? What did you say? Resist judging yourself, just observe.

Colleague

Think about someone at work with whom you work closely. In your next interaction with them, notice how they communicate, i.e. how rapid their speaking is, how they show you they are listening (or not), what questions they ask, and what statements they make.

Group   At one of your typical team meetings, pay attention to the group interaction instead of actively participating. (You can say that you just don't feel up to participating). Watch for the following: who speaks the most, the least; who seems to be influential, who does not; who listens well, who interrupts.

Strategy 7	*Increase awareness of "self-talk"*

Individual   Pick one day to write down most of the things you say to yourself. For example: "Don't forget to...", "I need to...", "I wish I hadn't said that..." Review the list of statements and note what themes emerge (e.g. To-Do's, Put-Downs). Are they past, present, or future-oriented?

Colleague   When you talk with others at work, what internal messages are you listening to? Are you attending more to your own "self-talk" than to the person who is speaking?

Group   During a faculty meeting, what are you saying or asking yourself that you are not saying aloud? Would any of these thoughts, if said aloud, result in improved communication?

Strategy 8   *Read with the purpose of understanding opposing points of view on a controversial issue*

Individual
Read two opposing letters to the editor. Imagine how each person came to his/her beliefs.

Colleague
Arrange with a colleague to read two articles with opposing points of view on a controversial subject (e.g. standard- based education, sex education, or inclusive education). Discuss your reactions to the opinions.

Group
Ask each person in the team, to read an article that presents differing points of view on a central theme (e.g. standards-based education, inclusive education, or assess-ment). Follow up with a team discussion regarding ideas and opinions.

Strategy 9   *Develop new ways to get to know your co-workers*

Individual
Think about something that you love to do outside of work which few of your colleagues know. Mention this to a few people in casual conversation.

Colleague
Ask a co-worker with whom you always meet at school to come to your home or to meet somewhere outside the school setting.

Group
Have each member on your team tell the group "One thing I did this summer for the first time."

Strategy 10 *Discover the importance of silence*

Individual
On your way to work, if you always have the radio on, turn it off. Consider other places where you can control the noise level.

Colleague
In conversation with a co-worker, observe whether or not there are silent periods. When you ask a question of your co-worker, be quiet until you are sure they have finished their answer.

Group
In a brainstorming session, have everyone stop for five minutes and write their ideas. After five minutes, resume the discussion.

Use this page to write down ideas that might come to mind while reading/referring to this guide.
Remember, collaboration begins with each one of us making ourselves accessible to others.

Section Four

ASKING QUESTIONS

It's better to know some of the questions than all of the answers.

James Thurber

ASKING QUESTIONS

What We Know

To ask questions is to inquire, to want more information, and to seek knowledge.

★ Asking questions demonstrates an interest in learning.

★ Posing questions with others can convey that we are open-minded.

★ To ask questions indicates a desire to move beyond the status-quo.

★ Pursuing answers to questions assists the development of our creativity.

★ People feel empowered when others show their interest by asking questions.

Asking Questions - What We DO

In asking questions

WHAT WE OFTEN DO with KIDS	WHAT WE SOMETIMES DO with ADULTS
Wait until we have their attention	Ask when *we're* ready
Ask open ended questions	Ask closed ended questions
Ask questions with the intent of gaining new information	Ask questions to be "polite"
Find several ways to ask the same question	Use limited variations of questioning
Ask a lot of questions	Make more statements than ask questions
Welcome most of their questions	Become defensive in response to some of their questions
Ask varying levels of questions (e.g. knowledge, understanding, analysis, synthesis, evaluation, opinion)	Ask questions mostly at the knowledge level
Join them in asking questions	Ask questions "at them"
Ask questions that prompt reflective thinking	Ask questions that require little reflection

Strategies for Asking Questions

1. Increase your awareness of questioning behaviors.

2. In conversations/discussions balance question-asking with statement making.

3. Learn to ask open-ended questions.

4. Develop questions related to what the speaker is addressing.

5. Find ways to inquire that are perceived as non-threatening.

6. Take opportunities to find the meaning of a message by asking questions.

7. Become aware of the intent of questioning.

8. Recognize the value of questioning.

9. Use questioning as a method of gaining support from your colleagues.

10. Share your philosophical questions with colleagues.

Strategies and Practices for Asking Questions

Strategy 1	*Increase your awareness of questioning behaviors*

Individual

Pick one day at work to listen for questioning behaviors among the adults with whom you work. In the lounge, hallway and classrooms, what kinds of questions are being asked?

Colleague

When you meet in a planning session with a colleague, do you ask many questions? What kinds of questions? When given an answer, do you typically accept it at face value or ask another question.

Group

At a faculty or team meeting where a new rule or policy is being discussed, have everyone write down one question they have about the policy. Read each one aloud to the entire group. Discuss the ones for which you have answers.

| Strategy 2 | **In conversations/discussions, balance question asking with statement making** |

Individual
After meeting with a co-worker, note how many questions you asked compared to how many statements you made. What's the difference between the two?

Colleague
Before meeting with a co-worker, decide that you will ask two questions to gain more understanding of what they are saying or thinking.

Group
Before an IEP staffing or child study meeting, have each team member write one question they have about the student. Post these questions so they are visible during the staffing.

| Strategy 3 | *Learn to ask open ended questions* |

Individual
Pay attention to the questions you ask others. Can most questions be answered with just one word or with "yes" or "no"? How could you change your questions so the responses would be more informative?

Colleague
In preparation for a parent conference, write down all of the questions you have about how the student feels about school. Review the list and cross off all questions that could be answered by "yes" or "no." Ask one or two of the remaining questions at the conference.

Group

Begin a staffing or child-study meeting by asking the parent "Would you please tell us about your daughter? What likes, dislikes she has? How does she feel about school?"

Strategy 4 ***Develop questions related to what the speaker is addressing***

Individual

As you listen to the principal speaking at a faculty meeting, write down questions that you have related to the topic. Note whether these questions are addressed.

Colleague

After a planning session with a co-worker, think about the questions that would have increased your understanding of your co-worker's ideas and suggestions. Try asking that type of question next time.

Group

At a committee or task force meeting, when you are tempted to state your feelings about what is being said, instead ask a question about what is being said.

Strategy 5 — *Find ways to inquire that are perceived as non-threatening*

Individual
Write down all the ways you could ask someone how they feel about an idea of yours. Which sound the least threatening to you?

Colleague
Rather than ask a co-worker why they do something, ask for them to tell you how they do something and what led them to that practice.

Group
Have team or committee members discuss ways to ask questions of parents that would not be perceived as threatening.

Strategy 6 — *Take opportunities to find the meaning of a message by asking questions.*

Individual
Listen to a talk show host for 15 minutes. Think of ques-tions you could ask him/her to further clarify what was said.

Colleague
When a colleague tells you about something they're doing with students, ask how or if it is different from what they did when they first started teaching.

Group
When you have a guest speaker in your class, listen closely for statements the students may not understand. Raise your hand and ask questions that will cause the speaker to explain more fully.

Strategy 7   *Become aware of the intent of questioning*

Individual

As you hear yourself ask questions to others, determine the purpose of the question. Are the questions for the purpose of gaining information, getting permission, criticizing, or making a request?

Colleague

Write down questions other people ask you. What did they need from your answer? Was it clarification, validation, explanation, or information?

Group

Team members often ask parents "Do you have any questions?" What is the purpose of this question?

Strategy 8   *Recognize the value of questioning.*

Individual

Once a month, write down all of the questions you have about yourself as a professional. Keep these in a journal and refer to them from time to time.

Colleague

Ask a colleague, "If you could create your own school, what would it be like?"

Group

At the end of a staffing or child study meeting, ask each person to express one question they still have about the student. Try not to answer these questions.

Strategy 9   *Use questioning as a method of gaining support from your colleagues.*

Individual   Think of something new you would like to try with your students. Ask a colleague to listen to the idea and provide feedback as to what the student response may be.

Colleague   After a lesson planning session with a colleague, seek out two other people on the faculty to see if they know of human or material resources that would enhance your lesson.

Group   When procedural changes are going to occur, have the faculty answer the question: "How shall we communicate this to parents."

Strategy 10   *Share your philosophical questions with colleagues*

Individual   Ask yourself "Why did I originally choose to enter this profession?" and then "Why am I choosing to continue in this profession?"

Colleague   Ask a colleague, "What is the most rewarding part of this job for you?" and "What is the most difficult?" Then share your answers with your colleagues.

Group   Read an article about student self esteem. Discuss the article in relationship to what each of you believes about self esteem.

Section Five

LISTENING

Nature has given us one tongue, but two ears, that we may hear from others twice as much as we speak.

Epictetus

LISTENING

What We Know

To listen is to make a conscious effort to hear what is being said.

★ When we listen well and actively, the communication is more efficient and effective.

★ Listening can increase our understanding of diverse perspectives.

★ When we are good listeners, others feel more accepted in our presence.

★ The better we listen, the more we have opportunities for meaningful connections with others

★ Listening is imperative to learning (we cannot learn if we do not listen).

LISTENING--What We DO

In listening

WHAT WE OFTEN DO with KIDS	WHAT WE SOMETIMES DO with ADULTS
Get down on their level (physically)	Remain on whatever level we begin the interaction
Give appropriate eye contact	Attempt to look at them and something else simultaneously
Attend well enough to ask questions related to what they just said	Attend enough so that we can make our next point
Allow the time they need to speak	Want their speaking pace to meet our needs
Listen for the feeling (emotions) behind the message	Take the words at "face value"
Watch for nonverbal cues along with what is said	Pay little attention to nonverbal cues
Give them our full attention	Attend to many things at once
Listen for messages/signs of understanding, growth, and change	Expect the messages to be of a "status quo" nature

Strategies for Listening

1. Learn to bring as much energy to listening as you do to speaking.

2. Establish routine checks to monitor listening behaviors.

3. Inform others when you need them as listeners.

4. Build listening times into established routines.

5. Learn to observe listening behaviors and their effects.

6. Increase awareness of selective listening.

7. Identify the barriers to effective listening.

8. Make conscious attempts to remove the barriers to effective listening.

9. Learn to attend to nonverbal messages.

10. Listen for the intent or purpose of a message.

Strategies and Practices for Listening

Strategy 1	*Learn to bring as much energy to listening as you do to speaking.*

Individual Identify settings where you tend to talk more than listen. Set a goal to increase your listening behavior in that setting.

Colleague In your next interaction with a co-worker, make a conscious effort to listen well enough so that you can ask a question to further understand what was said.

Group At a faculty meeting listen for and keep track of the number of questions asked as compared to statements made.

Strategy 2 — *Establish routine checks to monitor listening behaviors.*

Individual

During an evening at home, check every 30 minutes to note what was the last thing you heard. Are you listening more to internal noise (self-talk) or external messages?

Colleague

In conversation with a colleague, begin to note when you start to "tune out" their message. What causes you to tune out?

Group

During a faculty meeting, check your watch every 10 minutes and note whether or not you can repeat what was last said and who said it.

Strategy 3 — *Inform others when you need them as listeners.*

Individual

Think of a time when you just wanted someone to listen and instead they gave you advice. What could you say to them next time to prevent the advice giving?

Colleague

Think of ways to let another person know that you would appreciate their full attention as you tell them about an issue or concern.

Group

Before an interdisciplinary team meeting where parents will be present, ask you colleagues to listen for and record any jargon you use during your assessment report.

Strategy 4   *Build listening experiences into established routines.*

Individual
Take five minutes a day to stop what you're doing and just listen to the sounds in your classroom

Colleague
Record on audiocassette (with permission) a conference with a parent. When you play it back, listen for voice tone, interruptions, and the frequency and rate of speaking.

Group
Record a sample of a student speaking to the class. Play the recording for your team members and have them listen to and provide feedback on the student's speaking skills.

Strategy 5   *Learn to observe listening behaviors and their effects*

Individual
Notice the behaviors you like in a listener. How close do you want them to be? Do you like it when they nod in understanding? What behaviors make you feel you aren't being listened to?

Colleague
In an important discussion with a co-worker, how do you demonstrate that you are listening? What do you do that seems to result in the person telling you more?

Group
When you are speaking to a large group, what behaviors indicate to you that people are listening? What behaviors lead you to believe people are not listening? How does that affect your message?

Strategy 6 *Increase awareness of selective listening*

Individual
What radio stations do you listen to regularly? Why? What kinds of radio programs do you turn off? Why?

Colleague
When you talk with a co-worker, are there certain topics you listen to and remember? Are there other topics that you tune out almost immediately? Why?

Group
When discussing student progress, do you tend to listen better when others' results agree with yours? What happens to your listening skills when you hear results that conflict with yours?

Strategy 7 *Identify the barriers to effective listening*

Individual
Choose one day a week, for three weeks, and record events, people, or other distractions which interfere with your listening. Are they external factors or your own internal self-talk?

Colleague
What conditions in the school environment are interfering with effective listening during planning meetings with col-leagues? Write down the ones that you can do something about.

Group
As a team, ask "What is the one thing we could do to improve our listening to parents?" After these are shared, ask "What is keeping us from doing these things?"

Strategy 8   *Make conscious attempts to remove the barriers to effective listening*

Note: *These practices are directly related to strategy 7 practices 1-3*

Individual

Of the barriers identified in Strategy 7, Individual Practice Activity, which barriers are within your control to remove or reduce? If they are external barriers, take steps to make changes in the setting. If they are internal barriers, replace the interfering self-talk with messages like "Remember to listen. Are you listening? What did he just say?"

Colleague

Make a commitment to remove barriers identified in Strategy 7, Colleague Practice Activity. Let your colleagues know that you are doing this so that you can give them your full attention.

Group

As a team, set a goal related to improving listening to parents. Decide how you will keep track of your listening progress. Discuss your progress quarterly.

Strategy 9 *Learn to attend to nonverbal messages*

Individual

Turn on a favorite TV program. During the first five minutes watch the program with the volume turned down. Assess what you think is happening. Turn up the volume. Were you right?

Colleague

In a planning session with a colleague, notice the differ-ences in voice tone and gestures. Do they become more animated as they discuss certain aspects? How do they non-verbally demonstrate their interest in what's being discussed?

Group

During a team meeting, if you see someone looking as though they are confused or puzzled, follow-up with a ques-tion like, "Mary, do you have a question or a comment?"

Strategy 10 *Listen for the intent or purpose of a message.*

Individual

During a typical day, record the types of verbal interactions you have with your colleagues. Were the messages spoken for the purpose of polite social exchange, obtaining information, defending yourself or your opinion, explaining something, or just reporting?

Colleague

When people at work ask you "How are you?", do they have different reasons for asking the same questions? Which ones are just asking to exchange greetings and which ones want you to tell them?

Group

Think of all the messages sent during an IEP staffing. Write down the different types (assessment reports, progress data, developmental history, health status). Discuss with the team the perceived purpose of these messages. Do they help or hinder communication?

Use this page to write down ideas that might come to mind while reading/referring to this guide.
Remember, collaboration begins with each one of us making ourselves accessible to others.

Section Six

SPEAKING CLEARLY

It's not what you say, but how you say it that counts.

Robert Bolton
People Skills, 1979, Simon & Schuster.

SPEAKING CLEARLY

What We Know

To speak clearly is to send a message that is received
as we meant it to be.

★ When we learn to speak clearly we recognize that it is our responsi-bility to assure that effective communication has occurred.

★ Speaking clearly conveys a respect for the receiver and creates an atmosphere for mutual interaction.

★ When we learn to speak clearly, we learn to send messages that are more neutral in nature than judgmental.

★ The more clearly we learn to speak, the more likely the receiver will understand our message.

★ Learning to speak clearly will enhance the efficiency and effectiveness of our communication interactions.

Speaking Clearly--What We DO

In speaking

WHAT WE OFTEN DO with KIDS	WHAT WE SOMETIMES DO with ADULTS
Explain what we mean	Expect they'll understand what we mean
Use "I" messages	Use "you" or "they" messages
Tell them what we want or need	Keep our wants and needs to ourselves
Individualize our message based on student needs	Fail to consider the others' needs when we're speaking
Find many ways to explain ideas	Explain ideas in limited ways
Look for new vocabulary to enhance understanding	Use the "same old words" in communication
Vary our pace according to the situation	Proceed at a similar pace most of the time
Compliment them on their achievements	Fail to give them verbal recognition
Tell them when their behavior is having a negative effect	Tell someone else about their behavior

Strategies for Speaking Clearly

1. Learn to use "I" messages.

2. Take responsibility for your spoken messages to be understood as you meant them.

3. Learn to ask for feedback regarding your spoken messages.

4. Become aware of the tone of your spoken messages.

5. Make it a habit to check for understanding during communication interactions.

6. Expand your speaking vocabulary.

7. Assess the situations where you have something to say yet avoid speaking.

8. Find ways to bring your voice to situations where you have avoided doing so.

9. Become a frequent observer of your speaking behavior.

10. Identify and observe role models whose speaking you would like to emulate.

Strategies and Practices for Speaking Clearly

Strategy 1	*Learn to use "I" messages*

Individual

Keep a journal for a month, making entries at least twice a week. Note all the controversial issues, questions, and dilemmas that arise. After explaining the issue, complete these sentences: "In relation to (the issue) I feel..",
"I think...", "I believe. . ", "I'm going to . . ".

Colleague

When a co-worker speaks negatively about to you about someone else and it makes you uncomfortable, say some-thing like "Hmm, I really haven't experienced her in that way."

Group

Think about an aspect of your team or committee work that you do not believe is very effective. Bring it up at your next meeting by prefacing it with something like "I need to talk with you about _____ and get your ideas on how to improve our meetings."

Strategy 2 *Take responsibility for your spoken messages being understood as you mean them.*

Individual

Think about the way you express yourself when you are in a stressful situation. What are all the possible ways you might be misinterpreted? How could you begin to be clearer in those situations?

Colleague

In a discussion with a co-worker, after you've spoken at length about an issue, pause and ask something like, "It's important to me that I know if I'm making my ideas clear. Please tell me what your understanding is of what I've been saying."

Group

After an IEP staffing, arrange to meet with the parent(s) for 20 minutes or so. Tell them that the team is working on improving communication skills and you would like their help. Discuss their understanding of what was said during the meeting.

Strategy 3 *Learn to request feedback regarding your spoken messages*

Individual

Write down several ways to request feedback such as "How did you think I came across? Did you hear me use any jargon in my report? Did I smile at the meeting?"

Colleague

Identify someone you talk with frequently and with whom you feel comfortable. Tell them you are working a specific area such as speaking more slowly. Ask them to watch you throughout the week and provide you with feedback from their observations.

Group

When you speak to a large group, ask the group to fill out a brief, anonymous questionnaire about your presentation. For example, have them rank you in the following areas: Getting to the Point, Making Eye Contact, and Speaking Loudly Enough.

Strategy 4	**_Become aware of the tone of your spoken messages_**

Individual

Turn on a cassette recorder in your room for a day. When you play it back, listen for your voice tone, pitch, pace, and volume. What patterns do you notice?

Colleague

During a conversation with a co-worker, try varying your speaking tone. For example, slow down when you want to make a point, speak softly as you convey concern, more loudly when you feel strongly about something. Note how each variation feels and whether or not it helps to convey the meaning.

Group

Obtain permission to audio tape an IEP staffing. As you play it back, note your voice tone. How does it compare to others? What does your tone convey? Does it sound friendly, formal, authoritarian, or casual?

Strategy 5   *Make it a habit to check for understanding during communication interactions.*

Individual   Write down all the ways you might ask, "Are you understanding what I'm saying?" Which ones feel the most natural for you to say?

Colleague   Tell a colleague that you're working on speaking clearly so people easily understand you. Ask your colleague to let you know if you are using words or expressions which may be confusing to others.

Group   During an assessment report on a student, stop a couple of times and say something like, "I want to be sure I'm making myself clear. Does what I'm saying make sense and how does it relate to what you know about this student?"

Strategy 6   *Expand your speaking vocabulary*

Individual   Think of all the ways you can positively recognize someone else's efforts. Write them down; add to the list regularly.

Colleague   When you thank a colleague for something they've done, tell them specifically the effect their gesture had on you. For example, "Thanks for the note you left in my box. It made a hectic day a lot brighter."

Group   Brainstorm with a child study team the many different ways to describe a student's strengths. Keep the list posted or available for additions and use.

| Strategy 7 | **Assess the situations where you have something to say, yet avoid speaking.** |

Individual

For one week at school, keep a record of the times you've wanted to speak up during the school day but did not. Where were these incidents happening; with whom; what was the topic?

Colleague

In relationship to your colleagues, are there some with whom you rarely share your opinions? What keeps you from sharing them with others?

Group

What is your comfort level speaking in large groups? Do you speak up in faculty meetings? What types of large groups are you least or most likely to speak? Why is this? Do you have any desire to change?

Strategy 8   *Find ways to bring your voice to situations where you have avoided doing so.*

Note: *These practices are directly related to Strategy 7, Practices 1-3*

Individual

From the record developed in Strategy 7, Individual Practice Activity, choose one type of incident or one setting where you are going to speak up. Do it! Review later, "How did it feel? What was the effect?"

Colleague

Think of one colleague with whom you rarely share your opinions. Identify a topic that is important to you, but probably won't be controversial (e.g. recognizing student success). Tell your colleague that you've been trying to increase and expand the ways you recognize student success. Share some of your ideas and ask for their ideas.

Group

Choose one type of large group that you'd like to speak up in but are hesitant to do so. Plan to say something at the next opportunity. Write down what you'll say. Practice in front of a mirror at home. Do it!

Strategy 9   *Become a frequent observer of your speaking behaviors*

Individual

What speaking habits do you have that interfere with communication? Do you say certain words or phrases so frequently that they've become meaningless? (e.g. "uh", "you know what I mean", or "ya know.")

Colleague

In a conversation with a co-worker who usually starts the discussion? Who talks the most? When you speak do you get right to the point or tend to beat around the bush? Do you talk too much, not enough, or just enough?

Group

When you become a part of a group, what is the pattern of your speaking behavior? Do you speak up right away or wait before saying anything. Do you speak comfortably with a lot of people you do not know? Is it easy for you to move from person to person and find things to talk about?

Strategy 10 *Identify and observe role models whose speaking you would like to emulate*

Individual

Think of a personality (television, radio, movies) that you admire. What kind of voice do they have? Take an oppor-tunity to listen and observe their voice tone, gestures, facial expressions, clarity, and speed with which they speak.

Colleague

Identify a co-worker who you believe has effective com-munication skills. For about a week watch and listen for what it is that characterizes their speaking. Which of those characteristics could you improve? How?

Group

What speakers or teachers do you know that have been clearly outstanding? Identify the speaking traits that connect them with their audiences.

Use this page to write down ideas that might come to mind while reading/referring to this guide.
Remember, collaboration begins with each one of us making ourselves accessible to others.

Tip Cards for Effective Collaboration

You may reproduce this section as stated on the copyright page.

100 Ideas to
Reduce Stress and Increase Productivity
Daily in Your Life

Patty Lee, Ed.D.

Ten Tips for Each Topic:

Coping with Resistant Colleagues
Investing Rather than Expending Energy
Collaborating Effectively with Paraprofessionals
Disagreeing Tactfully
Using Nonjudgmental Language
Expressing Yourself
Asserting Yourself
Drawing Out the Best in Others
Not Taking Things Personally
and
Ten Suggestions for Tip Card Use

© Peytral Publications, Inc.

Ten Tips
for
Coping with Resistant Colleagues

✳ Find the points on which you agree; articulate those points.

✳ Remember it is often the message that is resisted, not necessarily the messenger.

✳ Volunteer to serve on a committee together.

✳ Sit next to the person, not opposite or across from them.

✳ Review students' records with your colleague.

✳ Find opportunities for your colleagues to "tell you more" about something.

✳ Show authentic interest in an aspect of their teaching.

✳ Tell your colleague why you chose education as a profession.

✳ Recognize that you cannot change your colleague, but you can change *your* response.

✳ Remember you are an advocate for kids and resistance is normal.

© Peytral Publications, Inc.

Ten Tips
for
Investing Rather than Spending your Energy

✳ Participate regularly in activities that renew you.

✳ Recognize what you <u>can</u> do and put your energy there.

✳ Realize your job is infinite - FOCUS is important.

✳ Say "thank you" when someone compliments you.

✳ Identify activities you put off and yet are so glad once you do them. Do these more often.

✳ Learn a new skill.

✳ Hang out with positive energy people.

✳ Learn to tell your own stories to children.

✳ Give a sincere and specific compliment to a colleague.

✳ Do not say "yes" when you mean "no".

© Peytral Publications, Inc.

Ten Tips
for
Collaborating Effectively with Paraprofessionals

✳ Start and end each day with the paraprofessional.

✳ Provide the paraprofessional with constructive feedback ASAP.

✳ Say "thank you" frequently for specific acts.

✳ Ask the paraprofessional how *you* can help.

✳ Demonstrate what you mean.

✳ Recognize the individual and unique contributions of each paraprofessional.

✳ Occasionally meet together away from the school or work area.

✳ Encourage the paraprofessional to keep a daily journal of activities, thoughts and feelings .

✳ Ask the paraprofessional what they would like to learn.

✳ Advocate for the paraprofessional's professional growth.

© Peytral Publications, Inc.

Ten Tips
for
Disagreeing Tactfully

* Find the points on which you agree and state them.

* Use the word "and" more frequently than "but".

* Post points of discussion on a flip chart. Note the areas of disagreement.

* Have each person write their opinion; read the opinions aloud.

* Find your own way of saying, "I disagree". e.g. "I see it differently."

* State your opinion about the topic, *not* the other person.

* Restate what you understand others to be saying.

* Think before you speak.

* Find support for your viewpoint.

* Recognize when you are willing to compromise and when you are not.

© Peytral Publications, Inc.

Ten Tips
for
Using Nonjudgmental Language

✳ Avoid using the words _always_ and _never_.

✳ Use "_yes, and_" rather than "_yes, but_".

✳ Ask people to tell you more; elaborate.

✳ Put as much energy into listening as you do speaking.

✳ Expect and welcome different points of view.

✳ Ask "_how_" and not "_why_".

✳ Give the ideas some "_think time_".

✳ Explain differences (rather than compare).

✳ Recognize your own "_need to be right_".

✳ Remember "_right_" is relative.

© Peytral Publications, Inc.

Ten Tips
for
Expressing Yourself

* ✳ Write down what you want to say.

* ✳ Practice expressing yourself to a friend.

* ✳ Visualize yourself speaking with confidence.

* ✳ Take a deep breath before you speak.

* ✳ Remember you may be speaking for others who share the same opinion.

* ✳ Record your speaking experiences in a journal.

* ✳ Observe others who speak up and note the qualities you admire.

* ✳ Tape record yourself stating your opinion about an issue.

* ✳ Listen to the tape recording and note where your voice is strongest.

* ✳ Write ten ways to express the same message.

© Peytral Publications, Inc.

Ten Tips
for
Asserting Yourself

* Use "I" statements

* Don't preface your statement with an apology.

* Identify your role models of assertiveness. Note the qualities you would like to develop.

* Recognize where your opinion is different; state it.

* Check out your understanding of others' messages.

* Don't put down another person's opinion; simply state your own.

* Remember you are disagreeing about an issue, not competing with the other person.

* Give yourself a time-out from the discussion. Regroup.

* Give a sincere and specific compliment to a colleague.

* Do not say "yes" when you really mean "no".

© Peytral Publications, Inc.

Ten Tips
for
Drawing Out the Best in Others

* Ask others for their ideas and opinions.

* Listen well enough to ask related questions about the topic.

* Request their help when brainstorming about a current issue.

* Check to see that you are understanding where they are "coming from".

* Share common interests.

* When you have questions or need to discuss an issue, ask when is the best time to meet.

* Compliment others in authentic and specific ways.

* Observe what times of day are best for individual interactions.

* Put as much energy into listening to others, as you do when speaking to others.

* Encourage others to expand or elaborate on topics which they initiate.

© Peytral Publications, Inc.

Ten Tips
for
Not Taking Things Personally

* Many statements are disguised as questions. You don't have to answer them.

* Ask for the meaning of the message to be clarified.

* The message usually says more about the speaker than about you.

* You are not responsible for the whole world.

* The speaker would probably say this to a number of people -you just happen to be the immediate receiver.

* Visualize a cartoon caricature of the person; don't take it so seriously.

* Reassure yourself like you would reassure a friend.

* Ask the person if they meant it the way you took it.

* Increase your response-ability not your responsibility.

* People are more often upset with the situation than with you.

© Peytral Publications, Inc.

Tips for Effective Collaboration
Suggestions for Use

✳ Photocopy the Tip Cards on colored paper, laminate and post.

✳ Select a Tip Card as a "Feature of the Month". Try one or two suggestions. Note the results.

✳ Use one of the Tip Cards as a topic for discussion at a faculty meeting.

✳ As a recognition tool, give Tip Cards to people who demonstrate these abilities.

✳ Design professional development goals related to the tips.

✳ Ask team, committee, or task force members to choose areas which they would like to improve.

✳ Practice tip suggestions with students first, then colleagues.

✳ Reflect on why some tips are easy for you and others more difficult.

✳ Write your own tips for something you want to improve.

✳ Keep a journal reflecting your progress toward your individual goals.

© Peytral Publications, Inc.

AFTERWORD

This book is written to stress the importance of conducting ourselves in a respectful and interdependent manner as we face the future and realize that we are all in this together for the good of the students. I hope this book has shed light upon the many strategies and practices that contribute to more collaboration among educators, parents, students, and community. Perhaps it has prompted additional ideas, which you are able to carry out in your particular setting. As educators we are positive role models for the students in our care and the way we communicate with other adults sets an example of effective commun-ication and productive problem solving for our students. Students are impressed by how they see us behave and in what they hear us say.

Effective Communication depends upon our implementation of the following of six components: *Developing Expectations, Preparing Ahead, Understanding Perspectives, Asking Questions, Listening,* and *Speaking Clearly.* When we are able to do all of these effectively, we contribute to an overall purpose of providing a healthy learning environment for our students.

A Note from the Author

It has been an absolute delight to write this book! I have taught classes, seminars, and workshops in collaboration and communication for 15 years, and my students continue to be my greatest resource. I am available to conduct workshops and staff development opportunities for school districts nationally and internationally. With over 30 years of experience as a Speech Therapist, Counselor, Educator, Special Education Director and as an Associate Professor, I would be happy to assist you with the development of collaborative practices in your unique setting.

Also, if you have additional ideas you would like considered for a future publication, please call or write to me at the address listed below. Best wishes and good luck!

Patty Lee, Ed.D.
Changing Points of View
P.O. Box 254
Drake, CO 80515
(303) 669-6355

GLOSSARY

CHILD STUDY TEAM - A group of general and special educators who meet regularly to review and discuss students who may be experiencing difficulty in school. In some settings this team serves as a pre-referral special education team. It may also be referred to as an Intervention Team, Referral Team, Teachers Assisting Teachers (TAT) team.....

COLLEAGUE - Any adult working in the school setting in the interest of students For the purpose of this publication, the words *Colleague* and *Co-Worker* are used interchangeably.

COMMITTEE MEETING - A meeting comprised of staff members working together to address a specific issue. Some school districts use additional terminology such as Focus Team, Curriculum Team, Site Based Management Team...

IEP - The Individualized Education Program that is a legal document developed for a student who qualifies for Special Education Services. Different states require different membership, but usually it includes: General Educator, Administrator, Special Educator, Parent, Student, and additional school personnel who have been involved in the assessment of the student.

INTERDISCIPLINARY TEAM - A team that is responsible for carrying out the identification of students who are eligible for Special Services. Often includes but is not limited to: General Educator, Special Educator, School Psychologist,

Nurse, Counselor, Various Specialists (Speech/Language, Occupational Therapist, and Social Worker.

STAFFING - A meeting held to develop an Individualized Educational Pro-gram (IEP). Usually attended by members listed under IEP. This meeting may also be referred to as an Assessment Summary Meeting, Initial IEP Meeting, IEP Information Session, IEP Placement Meeting.

Please remember that this is a library book,
and that it belongs only temporarily to each
person who uses it. Be considerate. Do
not write in this, or any, library book.

WITHDRAWN

Peytral Publications, Inc., is here to help you. If you have
questions, comments, would like to place an order, or request a
catalog, please contact us by mail, telephone, fax, or online.
We will be happy to assist you!

Peytral Publications, Inc.
PO Box 1162
Minnetonka, MN 55345

To place an order call toll free: 1-877-PEYTRAL
All other questions or inquiries
Telephone (952) 949-8707
FAX (952) 906-9777
E-mail HELP@pevtral. com

For the most current listing of new titles and perennial best sellers,
we encourage you to visit our secure web site at:

www.peytral.com